I wonder...
HOW DOES THE WIND BLOW?

Written by Andrew Langley
Illustrated by Stuart Trotter

WISHING WELL BOOKS

Why is the sea salty?

Millions of years ago, the sea was not salty. As time passed, pieces of rock from the land were washed out to sea by the rivers. Some of the rocks contained salt. The salt dissolved in the seawater.

Seawater is so salty that we cannot drink it. But the salt is still very useful to us. Most of the ordinary table salt that we put on our food comes from the sea.

In hot countries, people collect salt from the sea. They fill shallow pools with seawater. The sun evaporates the water, leaving the salt behind.

Salt makes seawater denser than fresh water. Because of this, we can float more easily in the sea than in a lake.

Where does the water in a river come from?

Some rivers begin as rain. Some begin as melting snow. The water trickles down to form streams. Some water soaks through the rocks and comes out lower down as a spring.

The springs and tiny streams from the hills join together and make bigger streams.

These big streams join into wide rivers, which flow down to the sea.

Where does the sun go at night?

The earth is spinning like a top in space. During a day and a night, it makes one turn. Only one half of the earth is facing the sun at a time. For that part of the earth, it is day. The other half is facing away from the sun. It is night there.

As the earth spins, the sunlit half moves into darkness. At the same time, the dark half moves into the sunlight.

Why do stars shine at night?

Stars are very hot balls of gas that give out light. They shine all the time. Our own sun is a star.

During the day we cannot see the stars because the sun is much brighter than the stars. But at night, there is no sunlight and we see the stars shining.

What is a shooting star?

There are many lumps of rock flying around in space. Sometimes one of these rocks hurtles toward the earth.

When the rock hits the layer of air around the earth, it is traveling very fast. The air rushing past the rock heats it up so much that the rock burns up. We see this as a streak of light flashing across the night sky.

Why is it warm in summer and cold in winter?

As well as spinning like a top, the earth travels in a circle around the sun. The earth is always tilted slightly to one side. When the northern half of the earth is tilted toward the sun, it is warmer there. This is the northern summer. At the same time in the south, it is winter.

As the year passes, the southern half of the earth is tilted nearer the sun, and summer arrives there. In the north, it is winter.

Why does the moon change shape?

We can see the moon at night because the sun shines on it. But only one side of the moon is lit. As the moon travels around the earth, we see different parts of this sunlit half.

The moon takes about four weeks to circle the earth. At first, we see only a tiny part of its bright side. The moon has a crescent (banana-like) shape, because the rest of the moon is dark and we cannot see it against the black night sky. Each night we see a little more of the lit side until we see the whole side of the moon lit up. Then the bright side turns slowly away.

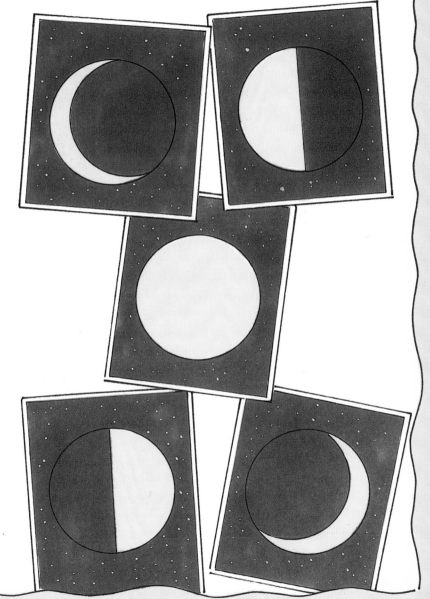

What makes the tide come in?

The moon is kept near the earth by a pulling force called gravity. The moon has its own gravity, too. It pulls at the earth and draws the oceans slightly outward on one side.

As the earth spins, the moon overhead pulls on different parts of the oceans. In this way, the ocean tides are "pulled" in and out.

What's at the bottom of the sea?

The bottom of the sea is not flat. The seabed rises and falls in deep valleys, wide plains, and high mountains, just like dry land. In some places, there are even underwater volcanoes.

Some parts of the seabed are very deep. The biggest valley is almost seven miles (eleven kilometers) below the surface of the sea.

The deep places on the seafloor look like a dark desert. Nothing grows here because there is not enough light.

There are many important metals in the depths of the sea. The most valuable of these is gold, which is dissolved in the seawater.

What is a rainbow?

A rainbow is an arch of color across the sky.

A rainbow happens when the sun shines on droplets of water. The water may be falling rain or the spray from a waterfall. You can only see rainbows if you stand with your back to the sun.

Though sunlight looks colorless, it is actually a mixture of many colors. The water droplets reflect the light and split it up again into its different colors.

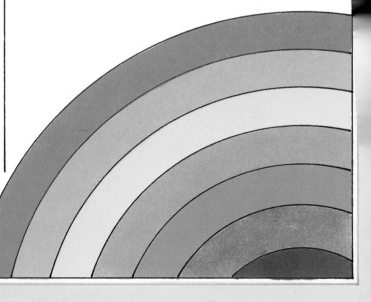

A rainbow has bands of color. They are violet, indigo, blue, green, yellow, orange, and red.

Why is the sky blue?

Light travels from the sun to the earth. Although the light seems to be white, it is made up of many different colors.

As the light moves through the air, the colors in it are scattered. The blue color is scattered most widely. That is why the sky looks blue.

Why are sunsets colored?

When the sun sets, we see its light through air that is near the ground. This air is often full of dust or smoke.

The dust scatters the yellow and red colors in the light so the sky looks yellow or red.

What are clouds made of?

When the sun shines, it warms the water in the seas, lakes, and rivers. The warm water turns into an invisible gas called water vapor. It rises up into the air.

As the vapor rises higher, it cools down. Some of it turns back into tiny droplets of water. Millions of these tiny droplets form a cloud.

Clouds come in many shapes and sizes. Stratus clouds are low and flat. Cumulus clouds are fat and puffy. Cirrus clouds are high and streaky.

Sometimes water vapor in the air cools very near the ground. It forms a low cloud that we call fog or mist.

What makes it rain?

A cloud is made of millions of tiny droplets of water floating in the air. If the air becomes cold, these water droplets sometimes join together. They form bigger drops. Soon they grow too heavy to stay in the air, and fall to the ground as rain.

What makes it snow?

Up in the highest clouds, the air is very cold. Any water vapor there freezes and turns into tiny crystals of ice.

If there are a lot of crystals in the air, they join together into flakes of snow. When they are heavy enough, they fall to the ground.

What causes lightning?

During a storm, the tiny water droplets in a cloud rub against each other. Each droplet becomes charged with a tiny amount of electricity. Because there are billions of droplets in a cloud, it has a huge charge of electricity.

When two storm clouds move close together, an electric flash jumps from one to the other. We call this lightning. Sometimes the lightning jumps down to earth, which is why you should head inside if you see lightning.

What is thunder?

As lightning flashes across the sky, the air near the lightning gets very hot. The hot air expands very quickly. As it rushes outward it bangs into the cold air nearby, making the air shake with a loud sound. This is thunder.

Thunder and lightning happen at exactly the same time. But light travels faster than sound. So we always see the lightning before we hear the thunder.

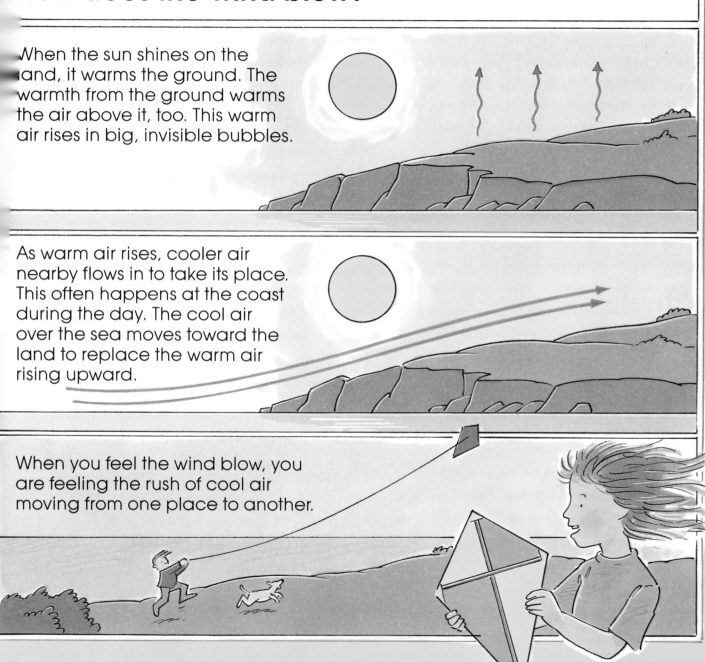

When the sun shines on the land, it warms the ground. The warmth from the ground warms the air above it, too. This warm air rises in big, invisible bubbles.

As warm air rises, cooler air nearby flows in to take its place. This often happens at the coast during the day. The cool air over the sea moves toward the land to replace the warm air rising upward.

When you feel the wind blow, you are feeling the rush of cool air moving from one place to another.

Where do icebergs come from?

On the high mountains in the frozen lands around the North and South Poles, snow falls all year round. The weight of the snow on top causes the snow underneath to turn into ice.

The ice becomes a huge frozen river. It slides very slowly down the mountain. This ice river is called a glacier.

When the glacier reaches the sea, huge pieces of ice break off and float away. These are icebergs.

Icebergs are a great danger to ships because only a small part of an iceberg can be seen above the water. Most of it is hidden underneath.

Why do volcanoes erupt?

Deep down in the earth, it is so hot that the rocks there melt and boil. The red-hot rock is called lava. A volcano forms where the lava has forced its way up through a weak spot in the earth's surface and flowed out above ground.

A volcano may erupt many times and throw out huge amounts of lava and ash. As the lava cools, it hardens and forms a cone shape.

Sometimes a volcano is blocked by a plug of hard rock. The heat and pressure underneath grows and grows. Suddenly, the volcano explodes with a massive bang.

Why do earthquakes happen?

The surface of the earth is made up of huge plates, like a jigsaw puzzle. These plates move very slowly in different directions.

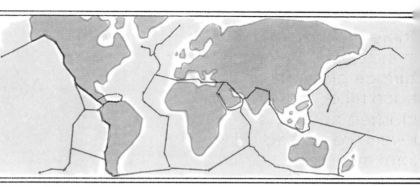

Sometimes the plates suddenly move faster and grind against each other. This makes the ground shake with great shock waves. We call them earthquakes.

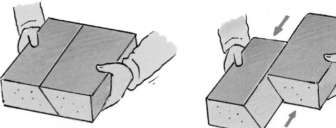

During an earthquake, the ground heaves and shakes. Most earthquakes do little harm. But some have caused whole cities to fall down.

If the earthquake is under the sea, it may set off massive waves. These race to the shore and can cause terrible damage.

ow are mountains made?

ere are many layers of rock
the earth's surface. When the
rface plates move toward
ach other, these layers are
ushed and folded. The folded
yers are pushed upward to
rm mountains.

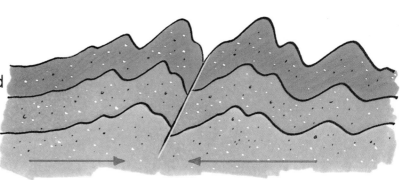

ther mountains may be
rmed by huge volcanoes.

Mountains never stay the same
or long. They are constantly
being worn away by streams
and glaciers.

GLOSSARY

A list and explanation of some of the terms used in this book.

Cirrus
— a thin, wispy type of cloud. Cirrus clouds are the highest kinds of clouds and may be about 52,500 feet (16,000 meters) above the ground.

Cumulus
— a fluffy type of cloud. Cumulus clouds are about 9,580 feet (3,000 meters) above the ground.

Eruption
— the violent explosion of a volcano.

Evaporation
— what happens when a liquid is heated and changes into a gas.

Glacier
— a huge river of ice that moves slowly down a mountain valley.

Gravity
— the force that pulls things toward the ground.

Iceberg
— a large piece of solid ice floating in sea.

Lava
— the hot, melted rock that flows out c volcano.

Stratus
— a low, flat type of cloud that covers sky in sheets and often brings steady ra

Volcano
— an opening in the earth's surface, through which lava and ash come up from the inside of the earth.

Water vapor
— liquid water that has been warmed turned into an invisible gas.